Big Cats

Leopards

by Marie Brandle

Bullfrog Books

Ideas for Parents and Teachers

Bullfrog Books let children practice reading informational text at the earliest reading levels. Repetition, familiar words, and photo labels support early readers.

Before Reading

- Discuss the cover photo. What does it tell them?
- Look at the picture glossary together. Read and discuss the words.

Read the Book

- "Walk" through the book and look at the photos. Let the child ask questions. Point out the photo labels.
- Read the book to the child, or have him or her read independently.

After Reading

- Prompt the child to think more. Ask: What did you know about leopards before reading this book? What more would you like to learn about them?

Bullfrog Books are published by Jump!
5357 Penn Avenue South
Minneapolis, MN 55419
www.jumplibrary.com

Library of Congress Cataloging-in-Publication Data

Names: Brandle, Marie, 1989– author.
Title: Leopards / by Marie Brandle.
Description: Minneapolis, MN: Jump!, Inc., [2021]
Series: Big cats | Includes index.
Audience: Ages 5–8 | Audience: Grades K–1
Identifiers: LCCN 2020023311 (print)
LCCN 2020023312 (ebook)
ISBN 9781645277231 (hardcover)
ISBN 9781645277248 (ebook)
Subjects: LCSH: Leopard—Juvenile literature.
Classification: LCC QL737.C23 B7247 2021 (print)
LCC QL737.C23 (ebook) | DDC 599.75/54—dc23
LC record available at https://lccn.loc.gov/2020023311
LC ebook record available at https://lccn.loc.gov/2020023312

Editor: Eliza Leahy
Designer: Michelle Sonnek

Photo Credits: Eric Isselee/Shutterstock, cover, 1, 3, 8, 14, 23m, 23br, 24; Minden Pictures/SuperStock, 4, 23tr; Avalon/Photoshot License/Alamy, 5, 23tl; apple2499/Shutterstock, 6–7; Biosphoto/SuperStock, 9; Maggy Meyer/Shutterstock, 10–11; Villiers Steyn/Shutterstock, 12–13; Chaithanya Krishnan/Shutterstock, 15; Chaiwat Photo/Shutterstock, 16–17; gifyster/Shutterstock, 18–19, 23bl; Sergio Sanchez Hernandez/Shutterstock, 20–21; Travel Stock/Shutterstock, 23bm.

Printed in the United States of America at Corporate Graphics in North Mankato, Minnesota.

Table of Contents

lair ····▶

A leopard guards her lair.
Why?

Her cubs are inside!

cub

Hyenas hunt the cubs.

hyena

paw

The mom growls.
She hits them.
Her paws are big.

8

The hyenas run.

It is safe.

The cubs come out.

They play!

They learn to hunt.

Leopards are big cats.
Cubs are still small.

They have spots.
We call them rosettes.
They are shaped like roses!

rosette

Spots help them hide in grass and trees.

15

These cats can swim.
They hunt fish
in the water.

Neat!

They hunt from trees, too.
They pounce on prey.
Wow!

19

They sleep in trees.
Sleep tight!

Where in the World?

Most leopards live in Africa. Some live in the Middle East and Asia. Take a look!

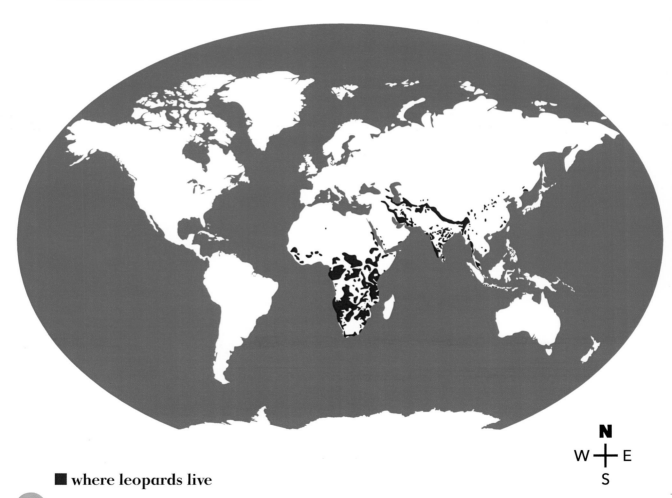

■ where leopards live

Picture Glossary

cubs
Young leopards.

growls
Shows anger by
making a low,
deep sound.

lair
A wild animal's
resting place
or home.

pounce
To jump forward
and grab something
suddenly.

prey
Animals that are
hunted by other
animals for food.

rosettes
Rose-shaped
markings on
the fur or skin
of some animals.

Index

To Learn More

Finding more information is as easy as 1, 2, 3.

❶ Go to www.factsurfer.com

❷ Enter "leopards" into the search box.

❸ Choose your book to see a list of websites.

24